50 Healthy Cereal Recipes

By: Kelly Johnson

Table of Contents

- Cinnamon Apple Oatmeal
- Chia Pudding Cereal
- Quinoa Breakfast Bowl
- Superfood Granola
- Almond Butter Oats
- Berry Chia Pudding Cereal
- Banana Nut Granola
- Coconut Quinoa Porridge
- Pumpkin Spice Oats
- Peanut Butter Crunch Cereal
- Hemp Seed Oatmeal
- Blueberry Almond Porridge
- Muesli with Dried Fruits
- Chia and Almond Butter Cereal
- Spiced Quinoa Cereal
- Maple Pecan Oats
- Coconut Yogurt Granola
- Baked Cinnamon Oats
- Protein-Packed Cereal Bowl
- Avocado Toast Cereal
- Apple Cinnamon Muesli
- Oats with Yogurt and Berries
- Poppy Seed Breakfast Porridge
- Tropical Granola Bowl
- Cranberry Almond Quinoa Cereal
- Choco Banana Oats
- Flaxseed Oatmeal
- Spiced Apple Quinoa
- Acai Berry Granola
- Greek Yogurt Muesli
- Mango Coconut Porridge
- Sweet Potato Oats
- Zucchini Noodle Cereal
- Raw Oat and Seed Bowl
- Almond Joy Granola

- Cashew Coconut Muesli
- Brown Rice Cereal with Almonds
- Apple Cranberry Granola
- Chia and Flaxseed Porridge
- Oats with Dark Chocolate
- Pomegranate Walnut Granola
- Avocado Chia Oats
- Date and Cashew Muesli
- Mixed Berry Oatmeal
- Maple Syrup Oats with Walnuts
- Pear and Almond Granola
- Sweet Cinnamon Quinoa
- Spicy Pumpkin Seed Cereal
- Coconut Almond Oats
- Tropical Fruit Cereal

Cinnamon Apple Oatmeal

Ingredients:

- 1 cup rolled oats
- 2 cups milk (or dairy-free alternative)
- 1 apple, peeled, cored, and chopped
- 1 teaspoon cinnamon
- 1 tablespoon maple syrup or honey
- 1 tablespoon chia seeds (optional)
- A pinch of salt

Instructions:

1. In a saucepan, combine oats, milk, and a pinch of salt. Bring to a simmer over medium heat.
2. Stir occasionally, cooking for about 5-7 minutes, until the oats are tender and the oatmeal thickens.
3. While the oats cook, heat a small pan over medium heat. Add the chopped apple, cinnamon, and maple syrup (or honey), and sauté for 3-4 minutes until the apples are softened and caramelized.
4. Stir the sautéed apples into the cooked oatmeal.
5. Optional: Stir in chia seeds for added texture and nutrition.
6. Serve hot and enjoy!

Chia Pudding Cereal

Ingredients:

- 1/4 cup chia seeds
- 1 cup almond milk (or any milk of choice)
- 1 tablespoon maple syrup or honey
- 1/2 teaspoon vanilla extract
- Fresh fruit (e.g., berries, banana slices)
- Granola (optional)

Instructions:

1. In a bowl, mix chia seeds, almond milk, maple syrup, and vanilla extract.
2. Stir well, cover, and refrigerate for at least 4 hours or overnight to allow the chia seeds to absorb the liquid and thicken.
3. In the morning, give the pudding a good stir.
4. Top with fresh fruit and granola for crunch.
5. Serve chilled or at room temperature.

Quinoa Breakfast Bowl

Ingredients:

- 1/2 cup cooked quinoa
- 1/2 cup milk (or dairy-free alternative)
- 1 tablespoon almond butter or peanut butter
- 1 tablespoon honey or maple syrup
- 1/4 cup mixed berries
- 1 tablespoon chia seeds or flax seeds

Instructions:

1. In a small saucepan, heat the cooked quinoa and milk over medium heat for 2-3 minutes until warm.
2. Stir in almond butter or peanut butter and honey, mixing well.
3. Transfer the quinoa mixture to a bowl and top with mixed berries and chia or flax seeds.
4. Enjoy as a wholesome and protein-packed breakfast!

Superfood Granola

Ingredients:

- 2 cups rolled oats
- 1/2 cup almonds, chopped
- 1/2 cup pumpkin seeds
- 1/2 cup dried cranberries or raisins
- 1/4 cup chia seeds
- 1/4 cup honey or maple syrup
- 1/4 cup coconut oil, melted
- 1/2 teaspoon cinnamon
- A pinch of salt

Instructions:

1. Preheat the oven to 350°F (175°C).
2. In a large bowl, combine oats, almonds, pumpkin seeds, chia seeds, cinnamon, and salt.
3. In a separate bowl, whisk together the melted coconut oil and honey (or maple syrup).
4. Pour the wet ingredients over the dry ingredients and stir to combine.
5. Spread the granola mixture evenly on a baking sheet lined with parchment paper.
6. Bake for 15-20 minutes, stirring halfway through, until golden brown.
7. Let it cool before adding dried cranberries or raisins.
8. Store in an airtight container for up to 1 week.

Almond Butter Oats

Ingredients:

- 1 cup rolled oats
- 2 cups milk (or dairy-free alternative)
- 1 tablespoon almond butter
- 1 tablespoon maple syrup or honey
- 1/2 teaspoon cinnamon
- Sliced bananas or berries, for topping

Instructions:

1. In a medium saucepan, bring the milk to a simmer over medium heat.
2. Stir in the oats, cinnamon, and almond butter.
3. Cook for 5-7 minutes, stirring occasionally until the oats are soft and the oatmeal has thickened.
4. Stir in maple syrup or honey.
5. Top with sliced bananas or fresh berries before serving.

Berry Chia Pudding Cereal

Ingredients:

- 1/4 cup chia seeds
- 1 cup coconut milk (or any milk of choice)
- 1 tablespoon maple syrup or honey
- 1/2 teaspoon vanilla extract
- Fresh mixed berries (e.g., strawberries, blueberries)
- Granola (optional)

Instructions:

1. In a bowl, combine chia seeds, coconut milk, maple syrup, and vanilla extract. Stir well.
2. Cover and refrigerate for at least 4 hours or overnight to allow the chia seeds to soak up the liquid.
3. Once the chia pudding has thickened, stir it again.
4. Top with fresh mixed berries and granola, if desired.
5. Serve chilled or at room temperature.

Banana Nut Granola

Ingredients:

- 2 cups rolled oats
- 1/2 cup walnuts, chopped
- 1/4 cup sunflower seeds
- 1/4 cup honey or maple syrup
- 1/4 cup coconut oil, melted
- 1/2 teaspoon cinnamon
- 1/2 teaspoon vanilla extract
- 1 ripe banana, mashed

Instructions:

1. Preheat the oven to 350°F (175°C).
2. In a large bowl, combine oats, walnuts, and sunflower seeds.
3. In a separate bowl, whisk together melted coconut oil, honey, cinnamon, vanilla extract, and mashed banana.
4. Pour the wet ingredients over the dry ingredients and mix until everything is coated.
5. Spread the granola mixture on a baking sheet in an even layer.
6. Bake for 20-25 minutes, stirring every 10 minutes until golden and crispy.
7. Let it cool completely before storing in an airtight container.

Coconut Quinoa Porridge

Ingredients:

- 1/2 cup quinoa
- 1 cup coconut milk
- 1 tablespoon honey or maple syrup
- 1/4 teaspoon ground cinnamon
- 1/4 teaspoon vanilla extract
- Sliced fruit (e.g., mango, banana), for topping

Instructions:

1. Rinse the quinoa under cold water.
2. In a saucepan, combine quinoa, coconut milk, honey, cinnamon, and vanilla extract.
3. Bring to a boil, then reduce to a simmer. Cover and cook for 12-15 minutes, until the quinoa is tender and the liquid has been absorbed.
4. Remove from heat and let it sit for a few minutes.
5. Top with your choice of fresh fruit and serve.

Pumpkin Spice Oats

Ingredients:

- 1 cup rolled oats
- 2 cups milk (or dairy-free alternative)
- 1/2 cup pumpkin puree
- 1/2 teaspoon cinnamon
- 1/4 teaspoon nutmeg
- 1 tablespoon maple syrup
- A pinch of salt
- Chopped nuts or seeds for topping (optional)

Instructions:

1. In a saucepan, combine oats, milk, and a pinch of salt. Bring to a simmer over medium heat.
2. Stir in pumpkin puree, cinnamon, nutmeg, and maple syrup.
3. Cook for about 5-7 minutes until the oats are tender and the mixture thickens.
4. Remove from heat and serve. Top with chopped nuts or seeds for added crunch, if desired.

Peanut Butter Crunch Cereal

Ingredients:

- 1 cup rolled oats
- 2 cups milk (or dairy-free alternative)
- 2 tablespoons peanut butter
- 1 tablespoon honey or maple syrup
- 1/4 teaspoon vanilla extract
- 1/4 cup granola or chopped nuts

Instructions:

1. In a saucepan, combine oats and milk. Bring to a simmer over medium heat.
2. Stir in peanut butter, honey (or maple syrup), and vanilla extract.
3. Cook for 5-7 minutes, stirring occasionally until the oats are tender and thickened.
4. Remove from heat and serve topped with granola or chopped nuts for crunch.

Hemp Seed Oatmeal

Ingredients:

- 1 cup rolled oats
- 2 cups water or milk (or dairy-free alternative)
- 2 tablespoons hemp seeds
- 1 tablespoon maple syrup
- 1/2 teaspoon cinnamon
- Fresh fruit for topping (optional)

Instructions:

1. In a saucepan, bring water (or milk) to a boil. Add oats and reduce heat to low.
2. Cook for 5-7 minutes, stirring occasionally, until the oats are soft.
3. Stir in hemp seeds, maple syrup, and cinnamon.
4. Remove from heat and serve with fresh fruit or toppings of your choice.

Blueberry Almond Porridge

Ingredients:

- 1 cup rolled oats
- 2 cups almond milk (or dairy-free alternative)
- 1/2 cup fresh or frozen blueberries
- 1 tablespoon almond butter
- 1 tablespoon honey or maple syrup
- Sliced almonds for topping

Instructions:

1. In a saucepan, combine oats and almond milk. Bring to a simmer over medium heat.
2. Stir occasionally and cook for 5-7 minutes until the oats are soft.
3. Stir in blueberries, almond butter, and maple syrup.
4. Continue cooking for another 2 minutes, until the berries soften and release their juices.
5. Serve topped with sliced almonds for added crunch.

Muesli with Dried Fruits

Ingredients:

- 1 cup rolled oats
- 1/4 cup dried apricots, chopped
- 1/4 cup raisins or sultanas
- 1/4 cup sliced almonds or walnuts
- 1/2 cup yogurt or milk (dairy or non-dairy)
- 1 tablespoon honey or maple syrup (optional)

Instructions:

1. In a bowl, combine oats, dried apricots, raisins, and almonds.
2. Add yogurt or milk and stir to combine.
3. Let the muesli sit for at least 10-15 minutes, or refrigerate overnight for a softer texture.
4. Drizzle with honey or maple syrup if desired and serve.

Chia and Almond Butter Cereal

Ingredients:

- 1/4 cup chia seeds
- 1 cup almond milk (or any milk of choice)
- 1 tablespoon almond butter
- 1 tablespoon maple syrup
- Sliced banana or berries for topping

Instructions:

1. In a bowl, mix chia seeds, almond milk, almond butter, and maple syrup.
2. Stir well, cover, and refrigerate for at least 4 hours or overnight to thicken.
3. Stir the chia mixture before serving.
4. Top with sliced banana or berries for a healthy and satisfying breakfast.

Spiced Quinoa Cereal

Ingredients:

- 1/2 cup cooked quinoa
- 1 cup milk (or dairy-free alternative)
- 1/2 teaspoon cinnamon
- 1/4 teaspoon nutmeg
- 1 tablespoon maple syrup
- Chopped nuts or dried fruit for topping

Instructions:

1. In a saucepan, combine cooked quinoa and milk. Bring to a simmer over medium heat.
2. Stir in cinnamon, nutmeg, and maple syrup.
3. Cook for 3-5 minutes until the quinoa is warm and slightly thickened.
4. Serve topped with chopped nuts or dried fruit for added texture.

Maple Pecan Oats

Ingredients:

- 1 cup rolled oats
- 2 cups milk (or dairy-free alternative)
- 1/4 cup chopped pecans
- 1 tablespoon maple syrup
- 1/2 teaspoon vanilla extract

Instructions:

1. In a saucepan, combine oats and milk. Bring to a simmer over medium heat.
2. Stir occasionally and cook for 5-7 minutes until the oats are tender and thickened.
3. Stir in chopped pecans, maple syrup, and vanilla extract.
4. Serve hot and enjoy!

Coconut Yogurt Granola

Ingredients:

- 1 cup granola
- 1/2 cup coconut yogurt (or regular yogurt)
- 1 tablespoon shredded coconut
- 1/2 cup mixed berries

Instructions:

1. Spoon coconut yogurt into a bowl.
2. Top with granola, shredded coconut, and mixed berries.
3. Enjoy as a light and refreshing breakfast.

Baked Cinnamon Oats

Ingredients:

- 2 cups rolled oats
- 2 cups milk (or dairy-free alternative)
- 1 teaspoon cinnamon
- 1/4 cup maple syrup or honey
- 1/2 teaspoon vanilla extract
- 1/2 cup chopped apples or berries (optional)

Instructions:

1. Preheat the oven to 350°F (175°C).
2. In a bowl, mix oats, milk, cinnamon, maple syrup, and vanilla extract.
3. Stir in chopped apples or berries if desired.
4. Pour the mixture into a greased baking dish and bake for 25-30 minutes, or until the oats are set and slightly golden.
5. Serve warm, topped with additional fruit if desired.

Protein-Packed Cereal Bowl

Ingredients:

- 1/2 cup rolled oats
- 1/2 cup Greek yogurt
- 2 tablespoons chia seeds
- 1 tablespoon almond butter
- 1/4 cup mixed berries
- 1 tablespoon hemp seeds
- A drizzle of honey or maple syrup (optional)

Instructions:

1. In a bowl, combine oats, Greek yogurt, chia seeds, and almond butter.
2. Stir until well mixed, then top with mixed berries, hemp seeds, and a drizzle of honey or maple syrup if desired.
3. Enjoy this protein-packed, nutrient-dense cereal bowl!

Avocado Toast Cereal

Ingredients:

- 1/2 cup rolled oats
- 1/2 avocado, mashed
- 1 tablespoon lemon juice
- 1/4 teaspoon garlic powder
- A pinch of red pepper flakes
- Salt and pepper to taste
- 1 tablespoon sesame seeds (optional)

Instructions:

1. Cook the oats according to package directions (with water or milk).
2. Mash the avocado and mix with lemon juice, garlic powder, salt, and pepper.
3. Once the oats are cooked, spread the mashed avocado on top.
4. Sprinkle with red pepper flakes and sesame seeds, if desired, for added flavor and crunch.

Apple Cinnamon Muesli

Ingredients:

- 1 cup rolled oats
- 1/2 cup almond milk (or milk of choice)
- 1/2 apple, diced
- 1/2 teaspoon cinnamon
- 1 tablespoon honey or maple syrup
- 1 tablespoon chopped nuts (optional)

Instructions:

1. In a bowl, combine oats and almond milk.
2. Add diced apple, cinnamon, and honey or maple syrup.
3. Stir well and refrigerate for 15-30 minutes or overnight.
4. Top with chopped nuts for an added crunch and enjoy!

Oats with Yogurt and Berries

Ingredients:

- 1 cup rolled oats
- 1 cup milk (or dairy-free alternative)
- 1/2 cup Greek yogurt
- 1/2 cup mixed berries
- 1 tablespoon honey or maple syrup (optional)
- Chopped nuts or seeds for topping

Instructions:

1. In a saucepan, cook oats with milk over medium heat until tender, about 5-7 minutes.
2. Stir in Greek yogurt and sweeten with honey or maple syrup, if desired.
3. Serve topped with mixed berries and chopped nuts or seeds for crunch.

Poppy Seed Breakfast Porridge

Ingredients:

- 1 cup rolled oats
- 2 cups milk (or dairy-free alternative)
- 1 tablespoon poppy seeds
- 1 tablespoon honey or maple syrup
- 1/4 teaspoon vanilla extract
- Fresh fruit for topping (optional)

Instructions:

1. In a saucepan, bring the milk to a simmer.
2. Add oats and poppy seeds, and cook for 5-7 minutes until the oats are tender and the porridge thickens.
3. Stir in honey or maple syrup and vanilla extract.
4. Serve with fresh fruit for added sweetness and nutrition.

Tropical Granola Bowl

Ingredients:

- 1/2 cup granola
- 1/2 cup coconut yogurt
- 1/4 cup diced mango
- 1/4 cup diced pineapple
- 1 tablespoon shredded coconut
- A drizzle of honey or maple syrup (optional)

Instructions:

1. In a bowl, layer the granola and coconut yogurt.
2. Top with diced mango, pineapple, and shredded coconut.
3. Drizzle with honey or maple syrup for a touch of sweetness.
4. Enjoy this tropical-inspired granola bowl!

Cranberry Almond Quinoa Cereal

Ingredients:

- 1/2 cup cooked quinoa
- 1/2 cup almond milk (or any milk of choice)
- 1/4 cup dried cranberries
- 1/4 cup sliced almonds
- 1 tablespoon maple syrup
- A pinch of cinnamon

Instructions:

1. In a saucepan, warm the quinoa and almond milk over low heat.
2. Stir in dried cranberries, almonds, maple syrup, and cinnamon.
3. Cook for 2-3 minutes until heated through.
4. Serve in a bowl and enjoy the nutty, fruity flavors of this quinoa cereal.

Choco Banana Oats

Ingredients:

- 1 cup rolled oats
- 2 cups milk (or dairy-free alternative)
- 1 tablespoon cocoa powder
- 1/2 banana, sliced
- 1 tablespoon chocolate chips or cacao nibs (optional)
- 1 tablespoon honey or maple syrup (optional)

Instructions:

1. Cook oats in milk over medium heat, stirring occasionally.
2. Once the oats are cooked, stir in cocoa powder and honey or maple syrup if desired.
3. Top with sliced banana and chocolate chips or cacao nibs.
4. Serve and enjoy the chocolatey, banana goodness.

Flaxseed Oatmeal

Ingredients:

- 1 cup rolled oats
- 2 cups water or milk (or dairy-free alternative)
- 1 tablespoon ground flaxseeds
- 1 tablespoon honey or maple syrup
- Fresh fruit or nuts for topping

Instructions:

1. In a saucepan, cook oats in water or milk over medium heat.
2. Stir in ground flaxseeds and sweeten with honey or maple syrup.
3. Cook for an additional 2-3 minutes until thickened.
4. Serve topped with fresh fruit or nuts for extra flavor and texture.

Spiced Apple Quinoa

Ingredients:

- 1/2 cup cooked quinoa
- 1/2 apple, diced
- 1/2 teaspoon cinnamon
- 1/4 teaspoon nutmeg
- 1 tablespoon maple syrup
- 1 tablespoon chopped walnuts (optional)

Instructions:

1. In a bowl, combine cooked quinoa, diced apple, cinnamon, nutmeg, and maple syrup.
2. Stir well and heat in the microwave for 30-45 seconds, or until warm.
3. Top with chopped walnuts for added crunch.

Acai Berry Granola

Ingredients:

- 1/2 cup granola
- 1 packet frozen acai puree (or acai powder)
- 1/2 cup mixed berries (fresh or frozen)
- 1/2 banana, sliced
- 1 tablespoon honey or agave syrup

Instructions:

1. In a blender, blend the acai puree with a splash of water until smooth.
2. In a bowl, layer the granola, acai puree, mixed berries, and sliced banana.
3. Drizzle with honey or agave syrup and serve.

Greek Yogurt Muesli

Ingredients:

- 1/2 cup rolled oats
- 1/2 cup Greek yogurt
- 1/4 cup milk (or dairy-free alternative)
- 1/4 cup mixed dried fruits (raisins, apricots, cranberries)
- 1 tablespoon chia seeds
- 1 tablespoon honey or maple syrup (optional)

Instructions:

1. In a bowl, combine rolled oats, Greek yogurt, and milk.
2. Add dried fruits, chia seeds, and sweeten with honey or maple syrup, if desired.
3. Stir well and let sit for 10-15 minutes for the oats to soften.
4. Serve chilled or at room temperature for a creamy, protein-packed breakfast.

Mango Coconut Porridge

Ingredients:

- 1/2 cup rolled oats
- 1 cup coconut milk
- 1/2 ripe mango, diced
- 1 tablespoon shredded coconut
- 1 teaspoon honey or maple syrup (optional)

Instructions:

1. In a saucepan, cook oats with coconut milk over medium heat until the oats are tender, about 5-7 minutes.
2. Stir in honey or maple syrup, if desired.
3. Top with diced mango and shredded coconut.
4. Serve warm and enjoy the tropical flavors of this creamy porridge.

Sweet Potato Oats

Ingredients:

- 1/2 cup rolled oats
- 1/2 cup mashed sweet potato
- 1 cup milk (or dairy-free alternative)
- 1/2 teaspoon cinnamon
- 1/4 teaspoon nutmeg
- 1 tablespoon maple syrup
- Chopped pecans or walnuts for topping (optional)

Instructions:

1. In a saucepan, cook oats with milk over medium heat until tender.
2. Stir in the mashed sweet potato, cinnamon, nutmeg, and maple syrup.
3. Cook for an additional 2-3 minutes, stirring to combine.
4. Top with chopped pecans or walnuts, if desired, for a crunchy finish.

Zucchini Noodle Cereal

Ingredients:

- 1 zucchini, spiralized
- 1/2 cup Greek yogurt
- 1 tablespoon honey or maple syrup
- 1 tablespoon almond butter
- 1/4 cup granola
- 1/4 cup sliced almonds

Instructions:

1. Spiralize the zucchini into noodles and set aside.
2. In a bowl, mix Greek yogurt, honey, and almond butter until smooth.
3. Toss the zucchini noodles in the yogurt mixture.
4. Top with granola and sliced almonds for crunch and flavor.

Raw Oat and Seed Bowl

Ingredients:

- 1/2 cup rolled oats
- 2 tablespoons chia seeds
- 2 tablespoons pumpkin seeds
- 1 tablespoon sunflower seeds
- 1 tablespoon honey or agave syrup
- 1/2 cup almond milk (or any milk of choice)

Instructions:

1. In a bowl, combine oats, chia seeds, pumpkin seeds, and sunflower seeds.
2. Add almond milk and honey or agave syrup.
3. Stir well and refrigerate overnight to allow the oats and seeds to absorb the liquid and soften.
4. Enjoy a nutrient-dense, raw breakfast packed with seeds and fiber!

Almond Joy Granola

Ingredients:

- 2 cups rolled oats
- 1/2 cup sliced almonds
- 1/4 cup shredded coconut
- 1/4 cup honey or maple syrup
- 1/4 cup dark chocolate chips
- 2 tablespoons coconut oil
- 1/4 teaspoon vanilla extract

Instructions:

1. Preheat your oven to 350°F (175°C).
2. In a large mixing bowl, combine oats, sliced almonds, and shredded coconut.
3. In a small saucepan, melt coconut oil and mix with honey or maple syrup and vanilla extract.
4. Pour the wet mixture over the dry ingredients and toss to coat.
5. Spread the mixture evenly on a baking sheet and bake for 20-25 minutes, stirring halfway through.
6. Once cooled, sprinkle with dark chocolate chips and enjoy your Almond Joy-inspired granola!

Cashew Coconut Muesli

Ingredients:

- 1/2 cup rolled oats
- 1/4 cup cashews, chopped
- 1/4 cup shredded coconut
- 1 tablespoon honey or maple syrup
- 1/2 cup almond milk (or milk of choice)
- 1/4 teaspoon cinnamon

Instructions:

1. In a bowl, combine oats, chopped cashews, shredded coconut, and cinnamon.
2. Add almond milk and honey or maple syrup.
3. Stir to combine and let sit for 10-15 minutes to soften the oats.
4. Enjoy this nutty and coconut-packed muesli for a wholesome breakfast.

Brown Rice Cereal with Almonds

Ingredients:

- 1/2 cup cooked brown rice
- 1/2 cup almond milk (or any milk of choice)
- 1 tablespoon chopped almonds
- 1 teaspoon honey or maple syrup
- 1/4 teaspoon cinnamon

Instructions:

1. In a saucepan, heat the cooked brown rice and almond milk over medium heat until warm.
2. Stir in honey or maple syrup and cinnamon.
3. Serve the rice cereal in a bowl, topped with chopped almonds for a healthy, fiber-rich breakfast.

Apple Cranberry Granola

Ingredients:

- 2 cups rolled oats
- 1/2 cup dried cranberries
- 1/2 cup chopped apples
- 1/4 cup honey or maple syrup
- 1/4 cup coconut oil, melted
- 1/2 teaspoon cinnamon

Instructions:

1. Preheat the oven to 350°F (175°C).
2. In a bowl, combine oats, dried cranberries, chopped apples, and cinnamon.
3. In a small saucepan, melt coconut oil and mix with honey or maple syrup.
4. Pour the wet mixture over the dry ingredients and stir to combine.
5. Spread the mixture on a baking sheet and bake for 20-25 minutes, stirring halfway through.
6. Cool and store in an airtight container.

Chia and Flaxseed Porridge

Ingredients:

- 1/2 cup rolled oats
- 1 tablespoon chia seeds
- 1 tablespoon flaxseeds
- 1 cup almond milk (or any milk of choice)
- 1/2 teaspoon vanilla extract
- 1 tablespoon maple syrup (optional)

Instructions:

1. In a saucepan, combine oats, chia seeds, flaxseeds, and almond milk.
2. Cook over medium heat, stirring occasionally, until the mixture thickens to your desired consistency.
3. Stir in vanilla extract and maple syrup, if desired.
4. Serve warm and enjoy the nutrient-rich combination of chia and flaxseeds.

Oats with Dark Chocolate

Ingredients:

- 1/2 cup rolled oats
- 1 cup milk (or dairy-free alternative)
- 1 tablespoon dark chocolate chips or chopped dark chocolate
- 1 tablespoon honey or maple syrup (optional)
- 1/4 teaspoon vanilla extract (optional)

Instructions:

1. In a saucepan, cook the oats with milk over medium heat until the oats are tender and have absorbed the milk.
2. Stir in dark chocolate and allow it to melt into the oats.
3. Sweeten with honey or maple syrup, if desired, and add vanilla extract for extra flavor.
4. Serve warm, and enjoy the rich combination of oats and dark chocolate for a comforting breakfast.

Pomegranate Walnut Granola

Ingredients:

- 2 cups rolled oats
- 1/2 cup walnuts, chopped
- 1/4 cup pomegranate seeds
- 1/4 cup honey or maple syrup
- 2 tablespoons coconut oil, melted
- 1/4 teaspoon cinnamon
- Pinch of salt

Instructions:

1. Preheat your oven to 350°F (175°C).
2. In a large bowl, mix oats, chopped walnuts, cinnamon, and salt.
3. In a small bowl, combine melted coconut oil and honey or maple syrup.
4. Pour the wet mixture over the dry ingredients and toss to coat.
5. Spread the mixture onto a baking sheet and bake for 15-20 minutes, stirring halfway through.
6. After cooling, stir in pomegranate seeds for a sweet and crunchy addition.

Avocado Chia Oats

Ingredients:

- 1/2 cup rolled oats
- 1/2 avocado, mashed
- 1 tablespoon chia seeds
- 1 cup milk (or dairy-free alternative)
- 1 teaspoon honey or maple syrup (optional)
- Squeeze of lemon juice (optional)

Instructions:

1. In a saucepan, cook oats with milk over medium heat until the oats are tender and have absorbed the liquid.
2. Remove from heat and stir in mashed avocado and chia seeds.
3. Add honey or maple syrup for sweetness, if desired, and a squeeze of lemon juice for freshness.
4. Serve warm and enjoy this creamy, nutritious twist on your regular oatmeal.

Date and Cashew Muesli

Ingredients:

- 1/2 cup rolled oats
- 1/4 cup dates, chopped
- 1/4 cup cashews, chopped
- 1/4 cup dried cranberries or raisins
- 1 tablespoon chia seeds
- 1/2 cup milk (or dairy-free alternative)
- 1 tablespoon honey or maple syrup (optional)

Instructions:

1. In a bowl, combine oats, chopped dates, cashews, dried cranberries, and chia seeds.
2. Add milk and honey or maple syrup (if desired).
3. Stir well, then cover and let sit in the refrigerator for at least 4 hours or overnight.
4. In the morning, stir again and enjoy a hearty, nutty, and naturally sweet breakfast.

Mixed Berry Oatmeal

Ingredients:

- 1/2 cup rolled oats
- 1 cup mixed berries (fresh or frozen)
- 1 cup milk (or dairy-free alternative)
- 1 tablespoon honey or maple syrup (optional)
- 1/4 teaspoon vanilla extract (optional)

Instructions:

1. In a saucepan, cook oats with milk over medium heat until the oats are tender and have absorbed the liquid.
2. Add mixed berries and stir until the berries break down slightly and release their juices.
3. Sweeten with honey or maple syrup, if desired, and add vanilla extract.
4. Serve warm and enjoy the burst of berry flavor in each bite.

Maple Syrup Oats with Walnuts

Ingredients:

- 1/2 cup rolled oats
- 1 cup milk (or dairy-free alternative)
- 1/4 cup walnuts, chopped
- 2 tablespoons maple syrup
- Pinch of cinnamon (optional)

Instructions:

1. In a saucepan, cook oats with milk over medium heat until the oats are tender and the milk has been absorbed.
2. Stir in maple syrup and cinnamon (if using), and top with chopped walnuts for crunch.
3. Serve warm, and enjoy the sweet and nutty flavors of this comforting breakfast.

Pear and Almond Granola

Ingredients:

- 2 cups rolled oats
- 1/2 cup almonds, chopped
- 1/2 cup dried pear, chopped
- 1/4 cup honey or maple syrup
- 2 tablespoons coconut oil, melted
- 1/4 teaspoon cinnamon
- Pinch of salt

Instructions:

1. Preheat your oven to 350°F (175°C).
2. In a large bowl, mix oats, chopped almonds, cinnamon, and salt.
3. In a separate bowl, combine honey or maple syrup with melted coconut oil.
4. Pour the wet mixture over the dry ingredients and stir until well combined.
5. Spread the mixture evenly on a baking sheet and bake for 15-20 minutes, stirring halfway through.
6. Once cooled, stir in the chopped dried pear.
7. Store in an airtight container and enjoy a crunchy, nutty breakfast!

Sweet Cinnamon Quinoa

Ingredients:

- 1/2 cup quinoa
- 1 cup milk (or dairy-free alternative)
- 1 tablespoon honey or maple syrup
- 1/2 teaspoon cinnamon
- Pinch of salt
- Fresh fruit or nuts for topping (optional)

Instructions:

1. Rinse the quinoa under cold water and drain.
2. In a saucepan, combine quinoa, milk, cinnamon, and salt.
3. Bring to a boil, then reduce the heat and simmer for 15-20 minutes, until the quinoa is tender and the liquid is absorbed.
4. Stir in honey or maple syrup for sweetness.
5. Serve warm with fresh fruit or nuts on top for added texture and flavor.

Spicy Pumpkin Seed Cereal

Ingredients:

- 1/2 cup rolled oats
- 1/4 cup pumpkin seeds
- 1 tablespoon maple syrup
- 1/4 teaspoon cayenne pepper
- 1/4 teaspoon cinnamon
- Pinch of salt
- 1 cup milk (or dairy-free alternative)

Instructions:

1. In a saucepan, combine oats, milk, cayenne pepper, cinnamon, and salt.
2. Bring to a boil, then reduce heat and simmer until the oats are cooked and tender.
3. In a separate pan, toast the pumpkin seeds over medium heat until they start to pop and become fragrant.
4. Stir the toasted pumpkin seeds into the cooked oatmeal.
5. Drizzle with maple syrup for sweetness, and serve warm with a spicy kick!

Coconut Almond Oats

Ingredients:

- 1/2 cup rolled oats
- 1 cup coconut milk (or any milk alternative)
- 1/4 cup shredded coconut
- 1/4 cup sliced almonds
- 1 tablespoon honey or maple syrup
- 1/2 teaspoon vanilla extract

Instructions:

1. In a saucepan, cook the oats with coconut milk over medium heat until the oats are tender and the liquid is absorbed.
2. Stir in shredded coconut and sliced almonds.
3. Sweeten with honey or maple syrup, and add vanilla extract for extra flavor.
4. Serve warm and enjoy the tropical flavor of coconut and almonds!

Tropical Fruit Cereal

Ingredients:

- 1/2 cup rolled oats
- 1/2 cup pineapple, diced
- 1/2 cup mango, diced
- 1 tablespoon shredded coconut
- 1 tablespoon chia seeds
- 1 cup coconut milk (or any milk alternative)
- 1 tablespoon honey or agave syrup (optional)

Instructions:

1. In a saucepan, combine oats and coconut milk.
2. Cook over medium heat, stirring occasionally, until the oats are tender and the liquid is absorbed.
3. Stir in chia seeds and shredded coconut.
4. Remove from heat and serve topped with diced pineapple and mango.
5. Drizzle with honey or agave syrup if you prefer a sweeter breakfast.
6. Enjoy the bright and refreshing tropical flavors!

www.ingramcontent.com/pod-product-compliance
Lightning Source LLC
LaVergne TN
LVHW081338060526
838201LV00055B/2723